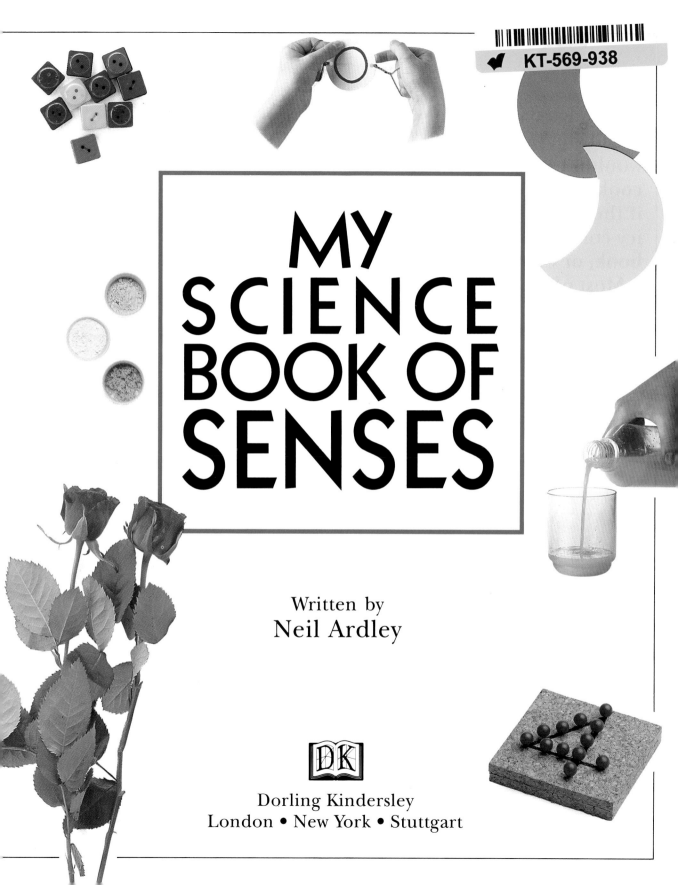

MY SCIENCE BOOK OF SENSES

Written by
Neil Ardley

DK

Dorling Kindersley
London • New York • Stuttgart

What are senses?

Your senses are your brain's link to the world you live in. Without them, you wouldn't hear music, or smell your dinner cooking in the kitchen. You wouldn't know if the air in the room was hot and sticky, or icy cold. You wouldn't be able to see this book, or even feel it to turn the pages.

Most of us have five senses: sight, hearing, touch, taste, and smell. They do not always work well. Some people cannot see or hear, for example. But we all use the senses we have to keep in touch with the world around us, and carry out the things we want to do.

Talking hands
People who lack one sense may use another to help them. Deaf people can "hear" messages in sign language.

Scent sense
Smells are mixed in with the air around us. To identify smells, we breathe or sniff in air to move it past smell detectors in the upper part of the nose.

DK

A Dorling Kindersley Book

Project Editors Scott Steedman and Laura Buller
Art Editors Christopher Howson and Peter Bailey
Production Louise Barratt
Photography Clive Streeter

First published in Great Britain in 1992 by Dorling
Kindersley Publishers Limited, 9 Henrietta Street, London
WC2E 8PS
Copyright © 1992 *illustrations* Dorling Kindersley Limited,
London
Copyright © 1992 *text* Neil Ardley

**British Library Cataloguing in Publication
Data is available**

ISBN 0-86318-684-X

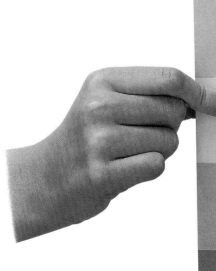

Reproduced in Hong Kong by Bright Arts
Printed in Belgium by Proost

On the ball

When you play games, you use your senses of sight, hearing, and touch. Good players use all these senses as well as they can.

Balancing act

Acrobats have to be good at balancing. You use your senses of sight, touch, and special parts inside your ears, to help you balance.

Bombarding the senses

Your brain gets lots of messages from your senses at a concert because of the bright lights and loud music.

⚠ This sign means **take care**. You should ask an adult to help you with this step of the experiment.

Be a safe scientist

Follow all the directions carefully and always take care, especially with glass, scissors, matches, candles, and electricity. Never put anything in your mouth or eyes. Do not do anything dangerous that could harm your eyes, ears, mouth, nose, or skin when you are testing your senses.

Inside the ear

How do you hear sounds? By making a model of an ear, you will see how your ears change sounds into signals that are sent to your brain. Your brain turns these signals into the sounds you hear.

You will need:

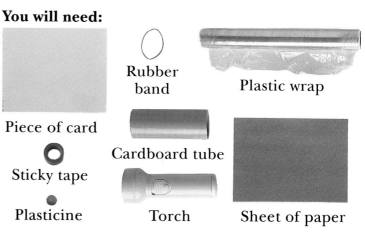

Piece of card

Rubber band

Plastic wrap

Sticky tape

Cardboard tube

Plasticine

Torch

Sheet of paper

The wrap must be smooth.

1 Stretch the plastic wrap over one end of the tube. Secure it with the rubber band.

2 Roll the sheet of paper into a cone and fasten it with sticky tape.

3 Tape the small end of the cone to the tube. This is your model ear.

Attach the card with plasticine.

4 Stand the card on a table top. Shine the torch on the wrap so that a spot of light appears on the card.

5 Shout or sing loudly into the cone. The spot of light shakes rapidly!

Sound waves make the plastic wrap wobble up and down. The light wobbles as well.

The hole in your ear is the opening of your "ear canal", a tube like the cardboard tube.

The wrap is like the "ear drum" at the end of your ear canal. It sends signals to your brain.

The cone acts like your outer ear and directs sound towards the hole in its centre.

Examining the ear
A doctor makes sure your ears are clean and healthy by looking into them with a special instrument. This device allows the doctor to see right down your ear canal to the ear drum.

Lost sounds

Why do we have two ears instead of one? Cover one ear and try to tell exactly where a sound is coming from. You'll soon know why we have two ears.

Cover one ear to block out sounds.

Using only one ear, we can't find the the source of a sound.

1 Use the cloth to blindfold a friend. Then ask your friend to cover one ear with a hand.

2 Move around the room quietly. Tap the two pencils together and ask your friend to point towards you. Your friend is usually wrong!

We can only hear where a sound is coming from if we hear it with both ears.

3 Ask your friend to listen with both ears and try again. Now your friend can point to where the sound is coming from every time.

Feeling right?

Your sense of touch tells you whether things are hot or cold. Or does it? See how something can feel both hot and cold at the same time.

You will need:

Three heat-proof glasses

Ice cubes

Cold water   Hot water

Add a little cold water if the hot water is too hot to touch.

1 ⚠ Fill one glass with hot water, and one with cold water and ice. Mix hot and cold water in the other glass.

2 Put one finger into the hot water and another into the iced water. Leave them there a minute.

3 Dip the hot finger into the warm water. The warm water feels cold, because it is not as hot as your skin.

You can tell only that something is hotter or colder than your skin.

4 Now dip the cold finger into the glass of warm water. The water feels hot!

Touch test

We easily feel things that touch our skin. Nerves in the skin detect them and tell us how hot or soft or painful they are. But how good is our sense of touch?

You will need:

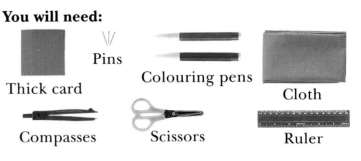

Thick card

Pins

Colouring pens

Cloth

Compasses

Scissors

Ruler

1 Using the compasses and ruler, draw three circles on the card, one inside the other.

The circles should be about 10 cm, 5 cm, and 2 cm across.

2 Cut out the large circle and colour the different zones.

3 Blindfold a friend with the piece of cloth.

4 ⚠ Stick two or three pins into the centre circle of the card. Make sure that the heads are level.

Make sure that no part of the card touches the skin.

5 ⚠ Gently press the pins against your friend's arm. How many pins can he or she feel? Next, test the palm and fingertips.

The nerves in the arm are spread out, so the skin is not very sensitive.

The palm is less sensitive because it contains fewer nerves.

The fingertips are very sensitive because the nerves in the skin here are close together.

6 Test again with pins stuck into the middle and then the outer circle. Your friend's arm will only detect all the pins when they are in the outer circle.

Making music

Playing an instrument like the saxophone needs great sensitivity of touch. Musicians use the lips and fingertips, which are among the most sensitive parts of the body.

Reading in the dark

Can you read without using your eyes? By using the fine sense of touch in your fingertips, you can read by feeling, instead of by sight.

You will need:

Cork tile   Scissors   Mapping pins   Pen   Cloth

1 ⚠ Carefully cut the cork tile into four squares with the scissors.

You could use part of your telephone number.

2 Draw a number on each cork square.

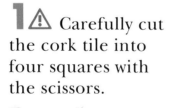

3 Stick mapping pins along the outline of each number.

4 Fold the cloth lengthways to make a blindfold. Use it to blindfold a friend.

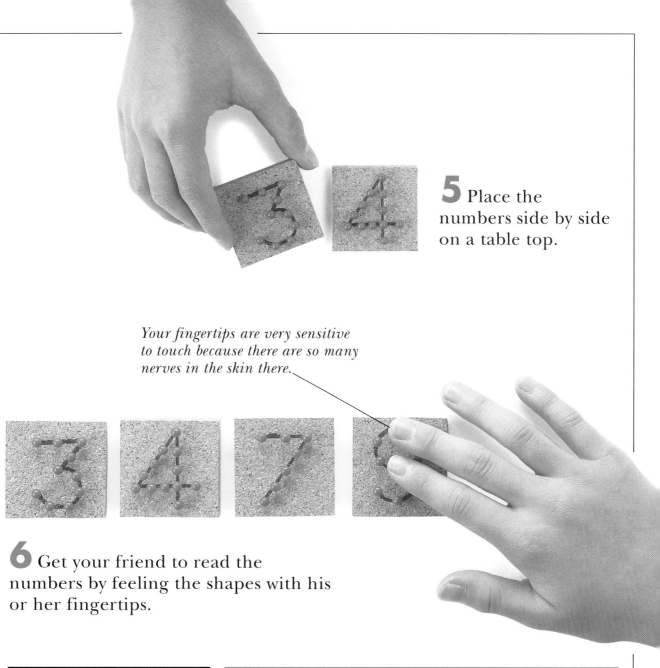

5 Place the numbers side by side on a table top.

Your fingertips are very sensitive to touch because there are so many nerves in the skin there.

6 Get your friend to read the numbers by feeling the shapes with his or her fingertips.

Books for the blind
Blind people read books that are printed in a special alphabet called "Braille". Each Braille letter is a pattern of raised dots. Blind people read by quickly running their fingers over the patterns of dots.

Inside the eye

How do your eyes see the world around you? Build a model eye, and see how light enters the eye and forms images. The images are turned into signals, which are sent to your brain.

You will need:

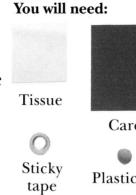
Tissue

Card

Torch

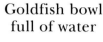
Goldfish bowl full of water

Sticky tape

Plasticine

Scissors

Magnifying glass

1 Tape the tissue to one side of the goldfish bowl.

2 Using some plasticine, stick the magnifying glass to the table top. This is your model eye.

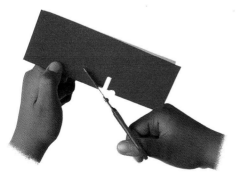

3 Fold the card in half and cut out half of a figure. Unfold it.

4 Use some plasticine to fix the card to the table top in front of the magnifying glass.

5 Place the torch in line with the figure and model eye. Switch it on. An upside-down image of the figure appears on the tissue. Move the magnifying glass back and forth until the image is sharp.

The round bowl acts like your eyeball.

You have a lens like the magnifying glass in each eye.

Light from the figure is bent by the glass to form an image on the tissue.

The tissue at the back of the bowl is like the "retina" at the back of the eye, where the lens forms an image.

When an image like this forms on the retina, signals go to your brain and you see the object.

Black hole

The dark hole at the centre of the eye is the pupil. Light passes through the pupil to reach the lens in the eye. The hole gets wider in weak light, to let in more light. In bright light, it becomes much smaller.

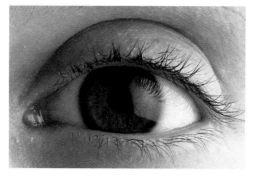

Cat and mouse

Stop a cat from catching a mouse, by making one of them disappear! This trick works because each of your eyes has a "blind spot". You cannot see any image which falls on this part of your eye.

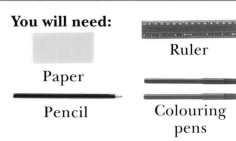

1 Make two marks on the paper about 8 cm apart.

2 Draw a cat by one mark and a mouse by the other.

3 Place a hand over your left eye. Stare at the cat as you bring the paper slowly towards you. The mouse suddenly vanishes! Then try staring at the mouse with your right eye covered. The cat disappears!

The retina has a spot that is not sensitive to light. If the image of the cat or mouse falls there, you can't see it.

Target practice

Why do we have two eyes, instead of one? Try to hit a target with one eye covered and you'll understand why.

You will need:

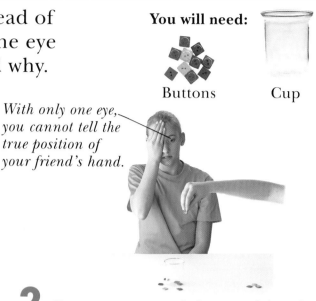

Buttons   Cup

With only one eye, you cannot tell the true position of your friend's hand.

1 Sit at a table with a friend. Place the cup in the middle of the table.

2 Cover one eye. Ask your friend to hold a button and move it about over the table. Say "Drop!" when you think the button is over the cup. You'll hardly ever get it right!

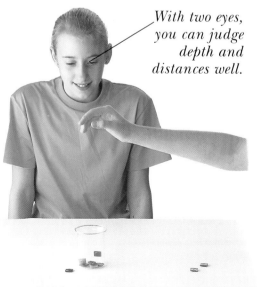

With two eyes, you can judge depth and distances well.

3 Try again with both eyes open. Your score will be much better.

Here's looking at you
An owl has two large eyes in the front of its head. These help the owl judge the position of its prey – and then catch it.

Two into one

Can you trick yourself into seeing two pictures as one? It happens because you go on "seeing" things for a short time after they go out of sight.

You will need:

Scissors

Compasses

Colouring pens

Two rubber bands

White card

Make sure the holes are directly opposite each other.

1 Using the compasses, draw a circle on the card. Then cut it out.

2 Make two holes near the edges of the card. Then draw a circle on one side.

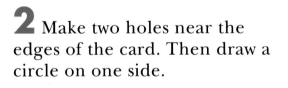

3 Draw a cross on the other side of the card.

4 Thread a rubber band through each hole.

5 Turn the card round several times until the rubber bands are tightly twisted.

You go on seeing the image of something for a moment after the object itself is out of sight. This is called "persistence of vision".

6 Release the card. It will whirl around, and you will see the cross inside the circle.

Because the card spins so fast, you see both sides at the same time.

Moving pictures

Movie films are long strips of photographs, each one slightly different from the one before it. A projector flashes these photographs rapidly, one after another, on to a screen. You see them combined, as a moving picture.

Seeing and believing

Can you always believe your eyes? What if they show you something you *know* is wrong? Make an optical illusion, and find out that sometimes your brain makes you see things that aren't there.

You will need:

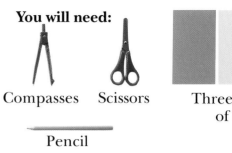

Compasses   Scissors   Three colours of card

Pencil

To draw the second circle, put the compass point on the edge of the first.

1 Use the compasses to draw two overlapping circles on one piece of card.

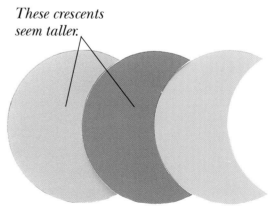

All three crescents are the same size.

2 Cut out the crescent shape. Trace around it on the other pieces of card and cut them out.

These crescents seem wider.

Your brain is confused by the way each crescent curves. They don't seem to be the same size.

3 Place the crescents in a line. Which one looks the biggest?

These crescents seem taller.

4 Change the order of the crescents. Now which one looks biggest?

Reaction ruler

Your senses warn you when you need to take action. Test your reaction time by catching a moving ruler. You will find out just how quick off the mark you are.

You will need:

Colouring pens

Glue

Paper

30 cm ruler

Scissors

Pencil

1 Draw around the ruler on the paper. Cut out the shape and mark six bands, each 5 cm long.

2 Colour the bands violet, blue, green, yellow, orange, and red. Then glue the paper to the ruler.

3 Hold out a hand. Ask a friend to suspend the ruler with the red end between your thumb and forefinger.

Keep your thumb and forefinger about 1cm apart.

4 Get your friend to drop the ruler without warning. Catch it! The colour you grab tells your reaction time.

Slow reaction time

Medium reaction time

Fast reaction time

Full of flavour

You can taste many different flavours in food and drink. But if you test your sense of taste, you will find that it's not just your mouth that tells one flavour from another. Your nose does a lot of tasting, too.

You will need:

Four different kinds of pure fruit juice

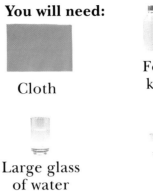

Cloth

Large glass of water

Four small glasses

1 Pour each fruit juice into a small glass.

2 Fold the cloth lengthways to make a blindfold. Use it to blindfold a friend.

It is easy to recognize each flavour.

3 Have your friend taste each glass of juice. Ask your friend to sip each one and say which juice he or she has just tasted.

4 Ask your friend to wash out his or her mouth between each tasting by drinking some water.

With the nose closed, it is hard to tell one juice from another. They all taste sweet.

We need to smell something as well as taste it, in order to recognize its flavour.

5 Try again, but this time ask your friend to hold his or her nose while tasting each juice. This time, it is not so easy to identify the juices.

A meal without appeal

Food does not taste very good when you have a cold. This is not just because you are feeling ill. You probably have a blocked nose. Your food seems to lose its flavour because you cannot smell it as easily as when you are healthy.

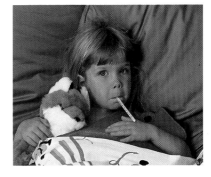

Nice and nasty

Bake some nice and nasty biscuits. Nibble them, and find out how tiny bumps on your tongue called taste buds help you to detect basic tastes.

You will need:

Mustard powder   Salt   Sugar   Plain flour

Baking sheet

Grated lemon peel

Tablespoon

Margarine

Paper towel   Rolling pin   Pastry board

Biscuit cutter

Three food colourings

Four bowls

Flour and sugar

Flour and salt

Flour and mustard

Flour and lemon

1 In each bowl, mix two tablespoons of flour and a tablespoon of one of these: sugar, salt, mustard powder, and lemon peel.

2 Add a tablespoon of margarine to each bowl and mix with your fingers.

Wash your hands between each bowl.

3 Add a different food colouring to three of the mixtures. Leave one mixture as it is.

4 Sprinkle flour on the pastry board. Roll out each mixture. Cut out biscuits with the cutter.

Wash the board, rolling pin, and cutter between each mixture.

Grease the baking sheet with a little margarine on a paper towel.

5 ⚠ Set the oven to gas mark 4, 350° F, or 180° C. Put the biscuits on the greased baking sheet and bake for about 15 minutes.

6 ⚠ Using oven gloves, take the biscuits out of the oven. Let them cool, then taste each colour of biscuit. Drink some water to wash your mouth between each tasting.

Each taste – mustard (bitter), lemon (sour), salt, and sweet – is detected by a different part of your tongue.

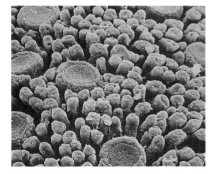

Taste detectors
This is a magnified view of the taste buds on your tongue. Parts of the tongue detect four basic kinds of tastes. You taste saltiness at the front, bitterness at the back, sourness at the sides, and sweetness over a large part of it.

Pot pourri

When we breathe in, smell detectors in our noses pick up different odours. Make a pot pourri and blend some sweet-smelling scents together.

You will need:

Saucer

Jar with lid

Cloves

Bowl

Baking tray

Paper towel

Roses

Teaspoon

Cinnamon   Lavender   Mint

The mint and roses will dry in two to three days.

1 Line the tray with a paper towel and cover it with the rose petals and mint. Put the tray in a warm, dry place.

2 Place the dried mint and rose petals in the jar. Add the lavender and a teaspoon of cinnamon.

3 Put the cloves in the saucer and crush them with the back of the spoon.

4 Add the crushed cloves to the jar. Screw on the lid and shake it well. This is your pot pourri.

Put your pot pourri in a bowl and let its scent fill the room.

5 Pour the pot pourri into a bowl. Smell it deeply! Its scent is a blend of flowers and spices.

Swell smell
Many flowers have a pleasant scent that attracts flying insects such as bees. The insects carry pollen from one flower to another. The plants need the pollen to produce seeds.

Picture credits
(Picture credits abbreviation key: B=below, C=centre, L=left, R=right, T=top)

Lupe Cuhna Photo Library/Vaughan Melzer: 6BR; Robert Harding Picture Library/Photri: 19BR; The Image Bank Schmid/Langsfeld: 25BR; David Rédfern Photography: 6BL;/Thomas Meyer:

13BR; Science Photo Library/Biofoto Associates: 9BL;/Dr Jeremy Burgess: 29BR;/Omikron: 27BL; Zefa Picture Library: 15BL;/K. Scholz: 7TR.

Picture research Kathy Lockley and Clive Webster

Science consultant Jack Challoner

Dorling Kindersley would like to thank Jenny Vaughan for editorial assistance; Mr Halpin, the staff and children of Harris City Technology College, London, especially Chad Calderbank, Andrea Charles, Elizabeth Dyer, Joel Edwards, Kristy Gould, James Jenkins, Chelene Jess, Amy Kelly, Faye Kester, Joanne McShane, Zoe Rooke, Raj Sudra, Emma White, Hing-Wai Wong; Sonia Opong and Ben Sells.